The American Southwest
Pride ~ Prejudice ~ Perseverance

Paulina Rael Jaramillo, M.A.

Enrique Pride
Pa. Ra. Jaramillo

BAEnd 2-9-11

<u>Special Acknowledgements</u>
Book cover/layout design by: Michele E. Bryer

Requests for permission should be sent to paulinajaramillo@charter.net.
Website: paulinajaramillo.com

ISBN: 1451558597
EAN-13: 9781451558593

To all the brave souls who came before us—

and in whose footsteps we follow —

and to those yet to come.

Author's Note

I have used the term Native American and Indian to refer to indigenous people living in North America; Spaniard to early American settlers from Spain; Mexican to citizens of Mexico; Mexican-American to U.S. citizens of Mexican ancestry; Hispanic to U.S. citizens who trace their ancestry to Spain and/or Mexico and other Spanish-speaking countries; Latinos to U.S. citizens who trace their ancestry to any of several Spanish-speaking countries; White-American and European-American to U.S. citizens of European ancestry; Chicano to Mexican-American students involved in the Chicano Movement.

Disclaimer

The territory (525,000 square miles) that was acquired by the United States from Mexico as a result of the Treaty of Guadalupe Hidalgo in 1848, included California, Arizona, New Mexico, Texas, Nevada, Utah and part of Colorado (see map page 25). However, this book covers only the regions that border Mexico. It is the author's intention to write a follow-up book that will include the areas not currently included.

Despite the epitaphs and labels denigrating their culture, despite history books ignoring their contributions and films portraying them as villains, Mexican-Americans cling tenaciously to their ethnic identity.

Despite changes, set-backs, deprivations and abuses, the Mexican-American—as an individual, as a family, as a diverse culture—relentlessly marches forward, empowered by centuries of survival.

The same unquenchable spirit that carried their predecessors to this land—carries them forward now.

SECTION ONE:

NATIVE AMERICAN, SPANISH AND MEXICAN PERIODS

"...by eliminating different civilizations and cultures, progress weakens life and favors death."

Octavio Paz

Introduction

In order to better understand the development of the North American Southwest, it is essential to comprehend, through a brief historical overview, the process of growth that each region underwent. Stereotypes that have evolved in one location of the Southwest tend to be randomly assigned to other locations, without consideration for the fact that each region developed with its own unique history. In an effort to avoid stereotyping, the author has chosen to discuss each state under a separate heading.

It is also important to note that the economic, social, religious and governing systems that were established by Native Americans and later by the Spanish and Mexican governments, gave way to new forms when the United States gained control.

The Native American Era

The American Southwest is a colorful tapestry woven with the various dialects, customs, cultures and architecture of the people who have dwelt in it for thousands of years. Some of the earliest recorded inhabitants are the Hohokam, Mogollon, Anasazi and the Fremont. They occupied the Four Corners area (Utah, Colorado, Arizona and New Mexico) as early as 300 BC (see map page 19).

The Hohokam constructed more than 500 miles of canals, some as wide as 75 feet across and several miles in length. They erected pit houses, lived in small communities and relied on hunting, gathering and farming as their food source. They are believed to be the ancestors of the Pima and the Papago.

The Mogollon built dwellings that were partially underground and used wooden beams for supporting the roof. They were skilled pottery makers and created wares that are regarded as some of the finest prehistoric pottery in the Southwest. After the Mogollon abandoned their villages they dispersed, most likely merging with other groups.

The name Anasazi came into use during the 1930's and was coined by archaeologists. It is thought that the Anasazi may have referred to themselves simply as "The People." They inhabited the canyons and mesas of the Southwest and constructed cliff dwellings and free-standing stone buildings (some as high as five stories). They developed various irrigation methods to counter the dry climate and grew corn, beans and squash. The Anasazi are considered to be the ancestors of the modern Pueblo people.

The Fremont inhabited parts of Colorado and Utah from 400 AD to 1350 AD. Archeologists believe they may have been a group of Anasazi that broke away and moved further north.

When the rainfall ceased and the ancient Native American population could no longer sustain itself, the dwellings were abandoned for more favorable conditions. Unlike Europeans, they did not lay claim to the land. They considered themselves to be custodians for Mother Earth.

When the Spanish explorers came to this region, they encountered well-organized and functioning societies of Pueblo Indians as well as deserted ruins.

Map of Ancient Civilizations
That Occupied The American Southwest

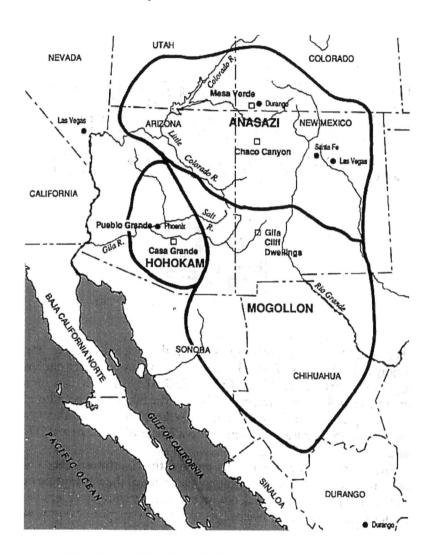

(www.cabrillo.edu/~crsmith/southwest.html)

The Spanish and Mexican Era

Before the Pilgrims, before the Founding Fathers and even before the United States itself, Spanish culture was alive and thriving in the region currently known as the American Southwest. Cabeza de Vaca, Friar Marcos de Niza and Francisco Vasquez de Coronado explored the mainland several decades before the English, French or Dutch. St. Augustine, the first North American town in Florida, was founded in 1565 by Pedro Menendez de Aviles. Starting in 1598, Juan de Onate explored the region that is currently New Mexico and Don Pedro de Peralta established the settlement known as Santa Fe (1609-1610). Both of these settlements predate the landing of the Mayflower in 1620 and the establishment of the Plymouth Colony by the English.

Although the Spanish explorers came seeking gold, many ended up as settlers, merchants, miners and planters. The practice of looting and exploiting indigenous people was not as successful in North America as it had been in the Southern region. Nevertheless, Spanish rule was imbued with caste privileges and, to a certain extent, dependent on peonage.

The Spaniards exerted their presence and authority over the native population through the establishment of *presidios* (military posts) and Catholic missions. The *presidio* served the purpose of providing security and protection against attacks by hostile Native Americans and became a base of operations from which to enforce Spanish dominance. Some *presidios* were small and guarded by a few soldiers. Others were large and protected by a regiment of cavalrymen. Most *presidios* were erected with building materials that were found locally (usually adobe and wood). They were typically built in a square or rectangular shape and had walls as high as ten feet. Circular *torreones* (large towers) were placed on two diagonal corners. They were used as lookouts and posts from which soldiers could fire their weapons. A typical *presidio* contained stables, storage facilities, a chapel and living quarters for officers and enlisted men.

Beginning in the sixteenth century, the missionary orders that came to Florida and the Northern region of Mexico (currently the American Southwest) were the

Franciscans, Dominicans, Augustinians and Jesuits. The Catholic Church was closely affiliated with the Spanish Crown, therefore the priests served not only as representatives of the church but also of the Spanish government. They labored to convert the native population to Catholicism as well as convince them to adopt the Spanish form of civilization, which they considered to be superior.

Most Native Americans had their own religious rituals and believed in a Supreme Being—a spiritual force as the giver and sustainer of life. Contact with European settlers tended to be abrasive and detrimental to their way of life. Many of them were enslaved and countless numbers died as a result of overwork and diseases.

When Mexico won its independence from Spanish dominance in 1821, all the territory along the northern region previously claimed by the Spanish Crown became part of Mexico. Unfortunately, the war caused immense destruction—crops and livestock were demolished and *haciendas* burned. Mines were left unattended and fell into decay. The new nation struggled to form a stable government and in 1824 adopted a federalist constitution. Dissension ensued between those who advocated a federalist government and those who favored a centralist government. This led to numerous civil wars and repeated changes in dictatorships.

Although Mexican authorities encouraged their citizens to colonize the frontier regions, Mexican settlement remained sparse. This weakened Mexico's ability to govern its frontier territories and encouraged *Tejanos* (Texans) to declare their independence from Mexico in 1836. The annexation of *Tejas* (Texas) by the United States nine years later, added fuel to the smoldering resentment that Mexico held against the United States for supporting *Tejas* in its fight for independence, and even more for its claim to superiority as demonstrated by the "manifest destiny" doctrine.

The situation escalated and in 1846 war was declared between Mexico and the United States. Although Mexicans were not financially prepared to withstand the assault of U.S. forces, they fought with boldness and courage. Unfortunately, Mexico's weaponry fell short of Mexican valor and in 1848 Mexico was compelled to sign a peace treaty at Guadalupe Hidalgo. The treaty assigned vast territories, approximately one-half the size of Mexico, to the United States (see map page 25). Mexico surrendered all claims to *Tejas* and the Mexican-American boundary was reestablished at the Rio Grande.

This signaled the end of Mexican domination of its northern provinces and the beginning of a new era in the American Southwest.

Territory Ceded by México
Under the Treaty of Guadalupe Hidalgo in 1848
and the Gadsden Purchase of 1853

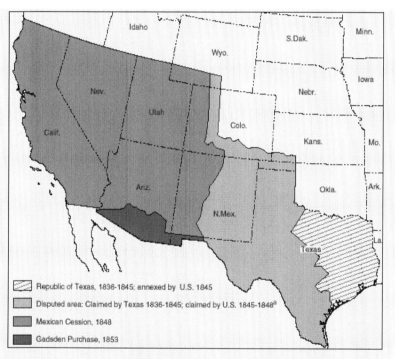

^aWhen Texas was officially recognized as a state in 1845, it included the light-gray area, which was also claimed by México. The Treaty of Guadalupe Hidalgo resolved this dispute, with Texas claiming the disputed land. In 1850, Texas transferred part of this land to the federal government, which became the eastern portion of the territory of New Mexico.

(United States General Accounting Office
GAO-01-330 Guadalupe Hidalgo Exposure Draft
http://www.gao.gov/new.items/d01330.pdf)

The Borderlands

Tejas/Texas

After the war of independence from Spain, the Mexican government was eager to populate its northernmost territories, and in 1823 granted permission to Stephen Austin to bring United States immigrants into *Tejas.* During the intervening years, he assisted more than 1,200 families to relocate. The settlers were required to become Mexican citizens, swear allegiance to Mexico and adhere to its laws. In turn, they were given land and exempted from tariffs for a period of seven years. The U.S. immigrants who settled in *Tejas* during the 1820's found the fertile soil ideal for cotton production. Before long, the new immigrants, many of them slave owners, greatly outnumbered the *Tejanos.*

This created concern in Mexico and caused the government to rethink its earlier decision. A law was enacted by Mexican officials in 1830 that prohibited further colonization of *Tejas* by settlers from the United States. The new law, along with Mexico's attempt to collect customs after the exemption period had expired, caused tension between the settlers and the Mexican government.

In 1836, Texas declared its independence from Mexico and gained brief status as a self-governing commonwealth—The Lone Star Republic. Nine years later Texas was annexed by the United States as a territory. Texas profited from Spanish and Mexican colonization in three ways: first, through the introduction of a Spanish system of land titles and other aspects of Spanish law; secondly, through the establishment of huge cattle ranches; and lastly, as a result of the lifestyle created by the Mexican *vaquero* (cowboy). According to the late historian J. Frank Dobie, everything that characterizes the American cowboy was acquired from the *vaquero,* including utensils, methods, vocabulary and equipment.

Texas economy was greatly dependent on cotton, cattle ranching and farming. Cotton plantations using slave labor were established mainly in the eastern part of the state. In 1861, Texas seceded from the United States and joined the Confederate States of America. During the Civil War, its main function was to provide supplies to the Confederate army. In 1870 it was reinstated into the Union. During the late 1800's, timber became an important commodity and in 1901, the discovery of petroleum ushered in the oil industry that became known as the "Oil Boom", which permanently changed the landscape and economy of Texas.

A new state constitution was passed in 1876 that allowed public school segregation. It was not until 1954, after the United States Supreme Court decision in *Brown v. Board of Education*, that school segregation was finally abolished. In 1902 the legislature passed a poll tax that voters were required to pay before registering. The tax caused participation by poor "Whites, African-American and Mexican-American" citizens to decrease significantly. The 24th Amendment ratified in 1964 abolished the poll tax at federal elections. However, it was not until 1966, after the United States Supreme Court ruling in *Harper v. Virginia Board of Elections,* that poll taxes for both state and federal elections were officially declared unconstitutional (Liberal Arts Instructional Services, 2010).

The United States House and Senate accepted the Texas state constitution in a joint resolution to admit Texas as a state on December 29, 1845, although the formal transfer of government did not occur until February 19, 1846.

New Mexico

Farming has been part of the landscape in New Mexico for centuries, first by the Pueblo Indians and their ancestors and later by the Spanish and Mexican colonists and their descendants. Cattle ranching and sheep raising have also played an important role in the state's economy due to the vast grazing ranges. New Mexico is also known for its mining industry and its own brand of artisans: weavers, smiths and wood carvers.

During the Spanish period the governing and social patterns in New Mexico were largely based on a semi-feudal system of land distribution. Landlords established themselves as *patrones* (masters) and ruled over the sedentary indigenous people who worked the land and were granted certain privileges in return (protection, shelter, food, etc.). The establishment of missions also played a significant role in the colonization of New Mexico. Approximately 25 missions were founded during the first century of settlement.

After the Mexican War of Independence from Spain, trade between the United States and Mexico increased enormously. The Santa Fe Trail became the hub of considerable commerce between the two nations. In the United States, the Santa Fe Trail (between New Mexico and Missouri) served not only to introduce certain commercial products, it ushered in progress and change. By the late 1860's, thousands of freight wagons loaded with manufactured goods were headed west each year.

When the Mexican-American War ended, New Mexico became a territory of the United States. According to Maurillio Vigil in his book, *Los Patrones,* when the American occupation began, a variety of reactions were displayed by the Hispanic political leaders. Some welcomed the new government, others saw it as an opportunity to pursue a new direction and others upheld their commitment to Mexico and opposed the intrusion. However, once the occupation became a reality, New Mexicans embraced territorial status.

Many reasons have been offered as to why it took New Mexico so long to become a state. Early efforts met with resistance partly due to ignorance regarding the territory and suspicions towards its inhabitants. Some viewed New Mexico's predominantly Hispanic and Native American population as being too foreign and too Catholic for admission into the American Union. Even the name of the state caused concern and resulted in periodic debates as to whether a new name would assist the cause of statehood (Torrez, 2010).

Finally, on January 6, 1912, President Taft signed the proclamation that admitted New Mexico into the Union as the 47th state.

Arizona

After the Treaty of Hidalgo was signed, disagreement between Mexico and the United States arose regarding exact boundaries. The U.S. wanted to have possession of the land south of the Gila River, which was also claimed by Mexico. The disputed area included the length of the southern portion of present-day Arizona and a section of New Mexico. President Franklin Pierce was eager to acquire the land in order to expand the railroad westward. Mexico wanted payment for damages incurred as a result of the U.S. failing to protect Mexican citizens on the frontier from marauding Indians, which was a stipulation of the Treaty of Hidalgo. The task of establishing the boundary line proved to be a challenging undertaking. Finally, President Pierce appointed James Gadsden as his emissary to Mexico to settle the dispute. In 1853, the Gadsden Purchase agreement was signed. The United States acquired an additional 45,535 square miles of land and Mexico acquired payment of $10 million.

Settlers throughout the Southwest experienced ongoing conflict with Native Americans. In Arizona only a handful of frontiersmen raised cattle. Although agriculture was limited, they managed to cultivate corn, wheat, barley and vegetables as well as fruit trees and grapevines.

The Indian raids that had deterred farming and ranching also deterred the development of a solid foundation in mining prior to the mid 1800's. James Officer in his book, *Hispanic Arizona,* states that in 1854 a group of speculators conducted an exploration in search of minerals in the Santa Rita Mountains. As a result, mining was reestablished and several Mexican and Mexican-Americans who had previously abandoned the mine returned. Among them were experienced men armed with specialized knowledge developed by their ancestors. This was the start of the indispensable contributions that Mexican-Americans would make in the development of Arizona's mineral industry.

On February 14, 1912, Arizona was the last of the 48 contiguous states to be admitted into the Union.

California

The missions played a significant role in the settlement of California. The Spanish monarchy wanted to establish a permanent settlement in the "New World" and sought to do so by building religious communities. The explorer Gaspar de Portola and Father Junipero Serra traveled to California in 1769 to set up the first of many missions. During a period of 54 years, 21 missions were established from San Diego to Sonoma spanning an area of 650 miles. The incentive was both political and religious. Spain wanted to claim ownership of the land in California before the Russians gained the upper hand by moving southward from Fort Ross (currently Sonoma County). They also wanted to convert the indigenous people to Catholicism while teaching them farming and other skills. Most of the Native Americans were treated badly by the Spanish soldiers and many of them died of diseases carried by the Europeans due to lack of immunity.

Living in the wealthiest of the borderlands, while being perhaps the most neglected subjects of the Spanish and Mexican governments, *Califorñios,* according to Gann and Duignan in their book, *The Hispanic in the United States,* began clamoring for regional autonomy, liberation from clerical dominance, separation between civil and military power and secularization of the missions. Most of these demands were obtained peacefully. By 1836 the *Califorñios* had their own form of government and were producing soap, wine and cloth for personal use. The *rancheros* raised sheep, horses and vast herds of hardy cattle. Sea merchants from the United

States and Great Britain exchanged dry goods, tools and other incidentals for larders of tallow and bales of hides.

The vast migration of White-Americans arriving in California from the 1840's on had no intention of assimilating into Mexican society and held strongly to the popular belief of America's "manifest destiny." Whatever remained of California's old social order was shattered as a result of the chaotic and mad dash that occurred during the gold rush of 1849. Although the Treaty of Hidalgo explicitly guaranteed existing property rights to Mexican landowners, the United States was unable and unwilling to honor them. Between the squatters who took possession of the land and the lawyers and politicians who questioned the *rancheros'* land titles in court, *Califorñios* soon found themselves impoverished. (By 1870 Mexican-Americans comprised only four percent of the population.) Many of them had gone from being wealthy landowners to being homeless in a country overrun by foreigners. Lawlessness and chaos abounded.

An essay titled, *The Lynching of Persons of Mexican Origin or Descent in the United States, 1848 to 1928,* published in *The Journal of Social History,* states that according to one estimate, approximately 25,000 Mexicans relocated to California between 1848 and 1852. Many of them were skilled and experienced miners and were able to mine gold in California successfully. However, their knowledge and ability were viewed as a threat by White-American gold miners who resorted to violence. It is estimated that between 1848 and 1860 no less than 163 Mexicans were lynched in California alone! (See page 38 for additional information.)

Flags from four nations have flown over California: Russia, Spain, Mexico and the United States. On September 9, 1850, California was admitted into the Union.

Inequality

By establishing and settling the Northern borders of Mexico (which later became the southwestern region of the United States) the Spaniards and Mexicans provided a foundation upon which to build. Their contributions ranged from politics to religion, from mining to farming, from works of art to sheep and cattle raising.

After the Treaty of Hidalgo was signed, the White-American population and their economic power increased. The 1860 census for Tucson, Arizona revealed assets owned by White-Americans amounted to more than $500,000.00, compared to less than $75,000.00 for "Hispanics." This was the rule rather than the exception throughout the Southwest.

A factor that helped create this type of economic imbalance was the manipulative methods of employment. In the interest of keeping operating costs down, the railroad and mines recruited Mexican and Mexican-American laborers who were willing to work long hours for little pay. Frequently, the wages were insufficient to cover living expenses and the miners became indebted to the company store that sold them supplies.

The practices of exploitation and coercion, which created deep resentments and ethnic distrust between cultures, was transferred into the social sector. Housing segregation and signs refusing service to people of Mexican descent were common throughout the Southwest. The criminal justice system created further alienation by issuing harsher and longer sentences to them than to White-Americans for the same crime.

This pattern of inequality penetrated into the political arena as well. The number of White-Americans in politics began to increase dramatically, while the number of Hispanics diminished during the latter part of the 19th century (with the exception of New Mexico). Although Mexicans and Mexican-Americans are not the only immigrants in the United States to have suffered abuse, the simple fact that the Southwest once belonged to Mexico adds a particular twist that Mexican sensibility finds difficult to accept.

Vigilantes and Lynching

In the introduction to an essay titled, *The Lynching of Persons of Mexican Origin or Descent in the United States, 1848 to 1928*, published in the *Journal of Social History*, William Carrigan and Clive Webb state the following:

> The lynching of persons of Mexican origin or descent has been largely overlooked by historians of American mob violence. This essay offers the first attempt to construct a systematic set of data on the subject. The authors contend that between 1848 and 1928, mobs lynched at least 597 Mexicans. Traditional interpretations of western violence cannot account for this phe-

nomenon. The actual causes of mob violence against Mexicans were several-fold: race and the legacy of Anglo American expansion, economic competition, and diplomatic tensions between Mexico and the United States. Throughout this era, Mexicans formulated numerous means of resistance against Anglo mobs. These included armed self-defense, public protest, the establishment of mutual defense organizations, and appeals for aid to the Mexican government. The central aim of this essay is to broaden the scholarly discourse on lynching by moving beyond the traditional limitations of the black/white paradigm. Placing the experience of Mexicans into the history of lynching expands our understanding of the causes of mob violence and the ways in which individuals and groups sought to resist lynching and vigilantism. The essay is based on numerous archival sources in both Spanish and English. These include diaries, letters, memoirs, folk culture, newspapers, government documents, and diplomatic correspondence.

Carrigan and Webb continue by stating that their essay *excludes* a significant number of reported lynchings because the sources did not allow for verification of specific data such as: dates, locations or identity of victim. Therefore, the statistics included in their essay should be considered conservative estimates of the actual figure.

SECTION TWO:

TURMOIL AND IMMIGRATION

"Here I stand, poor in money, arrogant with pride,
bold with machismo, rich in courage
and wealthy in spirit and faith."

Rodolfo Gonzales

Introduction

As a world of change, confusion and rejection was thrust upon Mexican-Americans, they pivoted to the two sources of strength that had served them well for centuries—the church and family. Even after the missions had begun to decline in the late 18th century, the Catholic Church continued to be a major influence, shaping the attitudes and behaviors of those in the community.

The family played a prominent role in their children's development by providing encouragement, acceptance, protection, discipline etc., as well as by being a positive role model. Although the economic, social and political institutions crumbled, the family structure survived intact, and from it Mexican-Americans derived a tenacious determination to prevail and even more—a desire to provide a better future for themselves and their children.

Conflict and Migration

By the start of the twentieth century, Mexico and the United States were worlds apart in their economic and social well-being, although they shared a border nearly 2000 miles in length. Torn by economic and political strife, Mexico struggled to survive as the government repeatedly changed hands from one dictator to another. The numerous revolutions, the economic and social upheaval, coupled with the need for laborers in the United States, became powerful incentives for migrating north. For many, the United States became a beacon of economic and/or social opportunity. For others, it offered refuge from oppression and turmoil. In many instances it was a means to gain both.

Like most immigrants from other countries, the majority of Mexicans who came to the United States were laborers. They contributed by their productivity and as consumers and tax payers. When they became financially stable many established businesses ranging from theaters to food markets and formed mutual aid societies and social clubs in their neighborhoods.

However, a significant number were artists, educators, engineers, lawyers, etc., who made valuable and lasting contributions in their respective fields. Oscar Martinez states in an essay titled, *Hispanics in Arizona*, that among the first massive wave of immigrants between 1910 and 1920 were a large number of middle and upper class people who were seeking to escape the chaos in Mexico. "Journalists, attorneys, physicians and businessmen from Sonora settled in Tucson's Mexican-American community, providing a needed infusion of new talent and leadership. In the years that followed (they) made a significant contribution through their professional work and involvement in civic activities."

Lured With False Promises

During the early part of the 1900's, labor agents from the United States actively urged Mexicans to migrate to the U.S. in order to fill labor quotas in industry and agriculture. They were promised adequate wages and decent housing. What they encountered instead were unhealthy and overcrowded living conditions and sub-minimal pay. Many were housed in barns and poorly constructed sheds. Their diet was meager, they were overworked, paid extremely low wages and were frequently cheated out of their earnings. Employers often resorted to pay advances and debts in an effort to retain laborers. In some instances migrant workers, who were housed in dormitory-like buildings, were locked in at night.

According to Marilyn Davis in her book, *Mexican Voices/American Dreams,* "Herbert Hoover, as czar of the United States Food Administration and chairman of major relief bureaus in Europe, saved millions of civilians and Allied soldiers from starvation during World War I." He boosted agriculture production by lifting restrictions that clogged the immigrant labor flow from Mexico. Immigration between 1910 and 1920 increased by more than 300 percent over the previous decade as thousands of Mexicans rushed to fill job vacancies left by enlisted men.

The immigrant laborers participated in railway construction and maintenance work in Southern California,

New Mexico and Nevada. In Texas they harvested cotton and vegetables. In California they labored in farms, citrus groves and orchards, as well as in canning factories, textile mills and various other enterprises. Their labor helped to enhance the economy of the Southwest and benefited the nation as a whole by maintaining food prices comparatively lower during and after World War I than in most other industrial nations.

Honor and Valor

The active participation of Mexican-Americans during wartime as enlisted men and civilian volunteers is impressive. Throughout most of the war history of the United States (from the Civil War to World War II and beyond) they have been quick to take up arms in defense of democracy.

During World War I, they enlisted voluntarily in greater numbers than any other ethnic group and served with honor and distinction in the Army and Navy. However, despite their dedication in the military and their support of the war on the home front, their loyalty was frequently doubted. In some regions of the country they were viewed as enemies of the United States.

Nevertheless, most Mexican-Americans remained strongly patriotic and in 1921 returning World War I veterans started a statewide organization in Texas called The Sons of America. The organization proclaimed commitment and patriotism to the United States and a desire to eliminate prejudice.

The organization was established in reaction to the growing racial discrimination and outright abuses that Mexican-Americans faced. Its initial focus was on civil rights, education and fair employment but soon expanded its agenda to include the fight for greater Hispanic political representation, health and economic issues. The Sons of America had several councils throughout Texas. In 1929 they merged with two other civil rights organizations, the Knights of America and the Latin American Citizens League. They adopted the name the League of United Latin American Citizens (LULAC).

LULAC grew rapidly and within the first three years of the merger, had expanded to Arizona, Colorado, New

Mexico, and California. It eventually extended its services into 48 states, Puerto Rico, Mexico, South America, and the armed service base in Heidelberg, Germany! According to a statement posted on LULAC's website the organization continues to improve conditions for Latinos:

> During its 80 years of history, LULAC has worked hard to bring many of the positive social and economic changes that Hispanic Americans have seen. Since then, LULAC has fought for voting rights and full access to the political process, and equal educational opportunity for Hispanic children. It has been a long and often difficult struggle, but LULAC's record of activism continues to this day...(through) voter registration drives and citizenship awareness sessions...health fairs and tutorial programs, and scholarship money for the LULAC National Scholarship Fund (www.lulac.org).

Deportation

As the prosperity of the 1920's gave way to the economic deterioration of the 1930's, the entire nation was greatly affected and most especially Mexican-Americans. They were forced to compete with White-Americans for jobs not only in urban areas but in rural settings as well. During the lowest point of the depression, they were unable to find work even in agriculture and factories due to falling prices and the large number of unemployed White-Americans seeking jobs.

Franklin D. Roosevelt's federal relief programs, although providing some assistance to Mexican-Americans, were overall less helpful to them than to the rest of the nation's poor. The reasons ranged from Mexican-American pride and reluctance to seek public assistance, to their inability to meet state residency regulations as a result of their migrant status.

Conditions during the depression fueled racial hatred to an all-time high. Anti-Mexican feelings were prevalent and expressed blatantly throughout the Southwest (especially in Texas) by various means, including signs stating, "No Mexicans or Dogs Allowed." In reaction to the continuing economic crisis, the government became increasingly desperate, culminating in an action that equals, if not surpasses, the infamy of the Japanese-American relocation during World War II. Between one-half to one million Mexicans and American citizens of Mexican descent were deported. Approximately 60% were U.S. citizens. The event took place with little regard for human rights and without due process. In some instances government officials did not bother to differentiate between Mexican nationals and Mexican-American citizens. In other instances, Mexican parents with American born children chose to take them rather than sever the family. Herbert Hoover, who had previously enticed Mexicans to the United States, sat in the Oval Office during the early 1930's and encouraged their removal.

A 2006 survey conducted by *USA TODAY,* found that only five out of the nine American history textbooks most commonly used in middle schools and high schools mentioned the deportation at all. Out of the five textbooks that did mention it, only one devoted more than half a page to the topic. While the same nine textbooks devoted a total of eighteen pages to the Japanese-American internment issue, a total of two pages were devoted to the forced Mexican-American deportation (Hunt, 2006).

Family, Coloñias and Unions

Even though deportation weakened and in some cases severed social and family ties, for the most part Mexicans and Mexican-Americans drew strength and courage from each other. Whenever possible they migrated to the United States with their nuclear and/or extended family and settled in pre-established Mexican-American *coloñias* (communities) or established their own.

The *coloñias* did more than reinforce Mexican culture and society. They contributed to the building of strong community cohesiveness and social organization. Mutual aid societies were organized almost everywhere they settled, for the purpose of providing sick and death benefits; social, patriotic and cultural activities; protection of civil rights and help in adjusting to life in the United States. C.C. Teague, who was associated with the Federal Farm Labor Board, is given credit for the following statement: "It is doubtful if laborers of this class of any other nationality take care of their own people who become incapacitated and impoverished as well as do the Mexican people."

The numerous patriotic celebrations and religious ceremonies that took place in most neighborhoods helped foster a vibrant cultural and social atmosphere that contributed to the development of Spanish-language movies, theaters, bookstores, restaurants and shops. The development of this unique environment came about by forces both internal and external. Internal, in that Mexicans chose to live close to each other and external, due to real estate segregation policies and discriminatory hiring practices. Although granted United States citizenship, Mexican-Americans were excluded from enjoying the full array of benefits, which further reinforced their tendency toward cohesiveness.

The family unit consisted not only of children and parents: grandparents, aunts, uncles and cousins often lived in the same household. Thus, close contact with a number of older relatives provided variety and made role modeling a powerful tool for learning. Children acquired survival, occupational and artistic skills, language, morals, etiquette, etc., and became familiar with Mexican history and folklore.

The celebration of life cycle rituals (birth, marriage and death) and devotion to the Catholic Church were essential features of the Mexican-American family and their social structure. The commemoration of life cycle rituals announced to the community the transition of individuals from one role to another and helped the persons involved to adjust. Cultural and religious festivities drew the society together and forged lasting bonds.

As a result of several factors, including family and social cohesiveness, juvenile delinquency among Mexican-Americans was not very prolific during this time period. Emory Bogardus in his book, *Mexican in the United States*, mentions that only 13.5 percent of the youth incarcerated in Los Angeles County in March of 1934 were Mexican or Mexican-American. From an early age on, children were indoctrinated with the importance of family honor and respect for elders. Rebellious youths were considered *malcriados* (badly brought up) and were seen as a negative influence by the *coloñia* as well as their peers.

By 1934, Mexican-American laborers in California had effectively organized some forty agricultural unions.

The most successful was the Confederacion de Uniones de Campesinos y Obreros Mexicanos (CUCOM) with 50 local chapters and 5,000 members. Among its goals were equal pay for Mexican-Americans and White-Americans performing the same job, cessation of job discrimination and limits on the immigration of Mexican laborers into the United States. Most of the unions were short lived. The use of violence to break up strikes and create disruption was a common practice that was used frequently throughout the United States during this time period.

Summary

The hope of a better future during a time when their own country was politically and economically devastated, coupled with the inviting promises from labor agents, lured many immigrants to the United States from Mexico. Once here they did their best to adjust to the conditions (in some cases appalling) and worked to improve their circumstance. Many joined the military and served their new country with honor. Due to job shortages during the 1930's, hundreds of thousands were deported back to Mexico with little regard for human rights.

The family, by aspiring to meet each others social, economic and educational needs, was in many respects a miniature version of society. It supplied physical and emotional necessities as well as basic education and moral training. The *coloñias* contributed to social and physical well-being and community cohesiveness. The church provided religious training and spiritual fortitude. All three institutions were crucial to the survival and welfare of the immigrants.

SECTION THREE:

WORLD WAR II, THE AFTERMATH AND THE CHICANO MOVEMENT

*"If you're outraged at conditions,
then you can't possibly be free or happy
until you devote all your time to changing them
and do nothing but that."*

Cesar Chavez

Introduction

The 1930's and the early 1940's was a frustrating and dismal period for Mexican-Americans. It started with mass deportation during the depression, continued with brutal suppression of efforts to unionize and culminated with the Zoot Suit Riots.

The 1960's and 1970's—known as the decades of social revolution—brought dramatic changes in society at large as well as changes within ethnic groups. Two powerful entities came into existence, each working to effect change in the Mexican-American community. The National Farm Workers Association improved immigrant farm labor conditions and the Chicano Movement made great advances in the equalization of civil rights.

The Bracero Program and World War II

In response to the labor shortage, the United States government introduced the Bracero Program in 1942. Mexicans under contract to American farmers were allowed to work in the United States. According to Camarillo, in his book *Chicanos in California,* over 150,000 braceros worked in farms, railroads and industries during World War II. Although the program was initially intended as a temporary measure, it continued for more than two decades. United States labor unions, politicians, Mexican-American leaders and Mexican government officials who were bothered by reports of contract violations and exploitations of their citizens, pressured the United States to terminate the program, which it finally did in 1964.

World War II and the years that followed brought both progress and disappointment to Mexican-Americans as they once again heeded the call to defend democracy. More than one-third million soldiers served in all branches of the armed forces. Raul Morin in his book, *Among the Valiant,* states that rural youth were volunteering and being drafted so quickly, in comparison with other ethnicities, that it created a labor shortage that caused farmers and ranchers to protest. Even Mexican nationals residing in the United States were not exempt. Many were recruited and later given the opportunity of becoming naturalized citizens.

Morin, who fought in World War II and spent several months convalescing in Army hospitals from war wounds, gives us a glimpse of the general attitude of many Mexican-American soldiers at that time. "We knew that there was something great about this country that was worth fighting for. We felt this was an opportunity to show the rest of the nation that we too were ready, willing and able to fight. It did not matter whether we were looked upon as Mexicans, Mexican-American, or belonging to a minority group; the war soon made us all genuine Americans."

Unfortunately, the majority of military personnel, ranging from officers to privates, did not see them as "genuine Americans." Instead, they continued to be viewed as second class citizens and were routinely assigned to the infantry regardless of their aptitude test scores. Service in the infantry often entailed assignments to the most hazardous combat duties. Approximately one-quarter of the combat troops positioned to defend Bataan in the Philippines were Mexican-American. Thousands who survived the battle died during the infamous Bataan Death March as a result of abusive treatment by their captors. The remaining survivors suffered a lengthy and wretched imprisonment.

Mexican-Americans were among the most decorated ethnic group in World War II. Thirteen men earned and were awarded the Congressional Medal of Honor for valor above and beyond the call of duty. Additional medals that were awarded included the Silver and Bronze Star, the Distinguished Service Cross and the Purple Heart.

The Zoot Suit Riots and the Fight for Equality

Ironically, while hundreds of thousands of soldiers fought and died for democracy overseas, their families were being oppressed and abused at home. On June 3, 1943, a rumor spread that Mexican-American men had beaten sailors over a situation involving Mexican-

American females. The newspaper headlined the rumor, causing sailors and marines (who had long resented the swaggering attitudes and style of clothes worn by the Zoot Suiters) to descend on the downtown Los Angeles area and into Mexican-American neighborhoods. They attacked local youth, beating them and stripping off their clothes, whether they wore Zoot Suits or not. The police turned a blind eye and the "Zoot Suit Riot" continued for five days. Finally, due to pressure from the Mexican Consulate, federal officials restricted Navy personnel from entering the downtown area and the riot ended.

After having actively participated in two World Wars, Mexican-Americans came away with new ideals and a renewed sense of power. Along with their medals and war wounds, they brought back an awareness of their political and economic rights as well as the realization of the widespread denial of those rights. The American G.I. Forum (AGIF) was established in Corpus Christi, Texas in 1948 by Hector Garcia, an army officer. Its initial purpose was to address the issues that veterans were facing by being denied medical services by the United States Department of Veterans Affairs.

In 1958, the forum became a national organization and currently intercedes in behalf of the rights of all veterans regardless of race, color or creed. The AGIF's focus has broadened to include a wide range of social and economic concerns in the Hispanic community and continues to promote education and the pursuit of higher learning.

The fight for equal rights had begun in earnest. It was to be a long and arduous battle. The practice of exploitation, segregation and discrimination had grown deep roots in American soil. Maltreatment of migrant workers was so blatant it elicited the following description of labor camps in 1934, by a commission appointed by the National Labor Board. "This report must state that we found...entire absence of sanitation and a crowding of human beings into totally inadequate tents or crude structures built of boards, weeds and anything that was found at hand...Words cannot describe some of the conditions we saw." Thirty years later those same conditions still existed!

According to Albert Prago in his book titled, *Strangers in Their Own Land: A History of Mexican-Americans,* wages for migrant workers in Texas during 1966 ranged from 40¢ to 80¢ per hour. (The federal minimum standard was $1.25.) Entire families, including children sometimes as young as seven, often had to work simply to put food on the table. They were excluded from protection under Child Labor Laws and from mandatory school attendance. The American Federation of Labor, which was instrumental in helping workers in existing unions, initially disregarded farm laborers.

The National Farm Workers Association

In 1962, Cesar Chavez and Dolores Huerta organized the National Farm Workers Association (NFWA). Their motivating desire was to help farm workers receive higher pay and improve their working conditions. A statement made by Chavez lends credibility to their desire. "If you're outraged at conditions, then you can't possibly be free or happy until you devote all your time to changing them and do nothing but that." From the beginning, the NFWA (later to become the United Farm Workers) adhered to the principals of non-violence. Chavez employed fasting and marches as a way of focusing attention on the cause.

His strong spiritual beliefs greatly influenced his dedication to peaceful reform. In 1968 he fasted for 25 days to show personal commitment, as well as the commitment of the farm labor movement, to non-violence. He fasted again in 1972 for another 25 days and in 1988, at the age of 61, he brought attention to the harmful effects of pesticides on farm workers and their families by fasting for 36 days.

The following statement shows his identification with the poor and suffering and his dedication to reform. "This solution to this deadly crisis will not be found in the arrogance of the powerful, but in solidarity with the weak and helpless. I pray to God that this fast will be a preparation for a multitude of simple deeds for justice. Carried out by men and women whose hearts are focused on the suffering of the poor and who yearn, with us, for a better world. Together, all things are possible."

On Mexican Independence Day in 1965, Cesar and the 1,200 members of NFWA voted to join a strike against the Delano grape growers. The strike had begun that month by members of the Agricultural Workers Organizing Committee (AWOC) who were mostly Filipinos. The fight was to last five years with the table grape growers, who used every means at their disposal to disband the picketers and discredit Chavez. Picketers were threatened, beaten, arrested, fired at, run-over, sprayed with pesticides, etc. In 1966, Cesar organized a march from Delano to the steps of the State Capitol in Sacramento in order to protest the ill treatment of the farm workers. The *peregrinación* (pilgrimage) started small but grew quite large as the marchers covered the 340 mile route. During the march and after a boycott that lasted four-months, Schenley Vineyards negotiated an agreement with the NFWA. It was the first union contract drawn up between a grower and a farm workers' union in the history of the United States.

Chavez placed great importance on the power of boycotting as evidenced by his statement, "The consumer boycott is the only open door in the dark corridor of nothingness...it is a gate of hope through which they (farm workers) expect to find the sunlight of a better life." Between 1967 and 1970, hundreds of strikers fanned out across North America and Canada to organize a national grape boycott. The boycott gained widespread attention and millions of Americans rallied, thus making it highly successful. It also gained the support of prominent figures such as Senator Robert F. Kennedy and Martin Luther King, Jr. In 1970, twenty-six growers who feared financial ruin and a bad public image, acquiesced to Chavez's demands, which included higher wages, improved living conditions and other concessions.

Lester Langley states in his book, *Mex-America: Two countries, One Future,* while agricultural workers benefited from the new contracts, their greatest victory was their success in touching the conscience of White-Americans and in alerting their compatriots of the lingering social and economic injustices.

The Chicano Movement

Motivated and inspired by the success of the farm workers in their fight for equality, thousands of Mexican-American university students in California initiated their own grassroots movement for social equality that became known as the Chicano Movement. The term Chicano became associated with youthful assertiveness and a civil rights agenda. Although students and their supporters also used the term in reference to the entire Mexican-American population, it nevertheless had a more direct application to the politically active movement.

Two major factors contributed to propelling the Chicano Movement forward—the questioning of traditional values and social norms that was taking place in the society at large and the increase of California's Mexican-American population which doubled between 1950 and 1960 (U.S. Census).

The Chicano Movement is diverse, multifaceted and compelling. It does not lend itself to a single definition or neat depiction. The Chicano initiative is composed of various goals. Many of them focus on education—the inception of bilingual/bicultural programs, development of Chicano centered curricula, increased number of Chicano educators and administrators, improved support services and many other educational issues. The movement also spearheaded cultural reform by creating politically motivated visual, literary and stage production art and addressing community concerns, employment issues and equality for women.

Throughout the 1970's, students numbering in the thousands formed several activist organizations. Although the leaders and participants in the movement did not always agree on policy and direction and indeed often quarreled, they had a common purpose—to acquire the civil rights and privileges that the larger sector of society already had. Eventually, most of them merged under the umbrella of El Movimiento Estudiantil Chicano de Aztlan (MEChA).

The movement achieved great advancements in higher education, employment and business and also won major civil rights victories but perhaps the greatest impact was on the people themselves. Mexican-Americans gained renewed strength and the realization of their ability to affect change. The general public became aware of them as a growing force with unstoppable power.

The movement is currently addressing concerns having to do with affirmative action and immigration.

Traditional Family/Changing Roles

Throughout history the nuclear and extended family has been a strong means of sustenance among Mexican-Americans. The communal family, apart from reinforcing culture, has contributed to the development of community cohesiveness and social organizations. Both family and community activities were closely linked to the Catholic Church. The observation of birth, baptismal and marriage rituals as well as religious and patriotic celebrations, were seen as both sacred and festive. Besides spiritual guidance, the church often provided physical and emotional sustenance.

However, the changes that are affecting the society at large are also affecting Mexican-Americans. The civil rights and feminist movements that began in the 1960's, the sexual revolution, increased mobility and urbanization, greater educational and employment opportunities, the emergence of a narcissistic culture with an emphasis away from family and religion, have all had a significant impact.

A prevailing characteristic of social reform has been the questioning of previously accepted norms. Although this can be a means of positive change, it often results in tension, dissatisfaction and distance between family members. This in turn creates a breakdown in communication at a time when communication is crucial. According to sociologists, children and youth are more likely to acquire maladaptive and delinquent behavior when they lack a healthy and supportive family structure and social identity.

Norma Williams in her book, *The Mexican-American Family: Tradition and Change*, states that in spite of the low assimilation rate of Mexican-Americans into the dominant culture, they are nevertheless being compelled to redefine their everyday lives in relation to the forces affecting society at large. She concludes, on the basis of her two-year research project conducted in Texas between 1981-1983, that the Mexican-American extended family has been disappearing. Among the economically advantaged in urban centers, the extended family is no longer central to everyday activities.

In addition, today's modern parishioner has a more casual attitude toward the church. A Catholic priest, who wishes to remain anonymous, feels that church attendance has become routine: "A nice place to go on Sundays."

Racial Identity and Assimilation

Despite the changes affecting Mexican-American families, however, Williams' research (1990) showed a continuing sense of ethnic identity and community cohesiveness. She contends that culture identification serves as a "buffer" against the adversity they face in society. Langley (1988) states the same thing in more explicit terms: "The lowliest Mexican fence jumper has a stronger sense of cultural identification than the American who employs him. He may not be able to read or write and have *nada de nada*, but he knows who he is and is not going to exchange his deeply felt sense of identity for something that neither America nor Americans have been able to define."

Assimilation of immigrants into a culture other than their own requires an economic, social and psychological transition that Latinos have been reluctant to make in the past. According to a national survey conducted by the Pew Hispanic Center (published in 2009) 41 percent of the native born children of Latino immigrants refer to themselves first by their parents country of origin, be it Mexico, Cuba, the Dominican Republic, El Salvador or any of more than a dozen other Spanish-speaking countries. Twenty-one percent use the terms Hispanic or Latino first and 33 percent of these young, second generation Latinos use the term American when referring to themselves. However, by the third and later generations half (50 percent) of the native-born Latino youth use American as their first term of self-description.

Although historically Latinos have tended to resist assimilation, it is too soon to tell if this process will continue for future generations of immigrants and their offspring. One thing is certain—Latino youth, like all young people everywhere, are facing a world that is becoming increasingly global, forcing them to come face-to-face with decisions their parents and grandparents did not have to make.

SECTION FOUR:
BEYOND THE CHICANO MOVEMENT

*"History, despite its wrenching pain,
cannot be unlived, but if faced with courage,
need not be lived again."*

Maya Angelou

Introduction

The first major wave of immigration into the United States began in 1840 and peaked during the early 1880's with slightly more than five million arrivals. The majority of immigrants came from Northern and Western Europe. The next wave occurred during the first decade of the 20th century with the arrival of approximately nine million immigrants, mostly from Southern and Central Europe. The highest numerical peak thus far occurred during the 1990's with nearly 10 million immigrants coming to the United States, most of them from Asia and Latin America.

Anti-immigrant Sentiments
in the 1960's through the 1990's

The Immigration and Nationality Amendments went into effect in 1965. It limited immigration from the Western Hemisphere (particularly Mexico). Paradoxically, it set the stage for the expansion of illegal immigration. Twenty-one years later, due to the increasing number of undocumented immigrants, the Immigration Reform and Control Act (IRCA) was established. It instituted employer sanctions for knowingly hiring illegal workers, increased border patrol and created legalization programs.

In 1993, fueled by Governor Pete Wilson's political campaign in California and the economic recession that was taking place, attention was focused once again on immigrants. Wilson, Senator Dianne Feinstein and other politicians would have us believe that the economic crisis was due to the presence of undocumented immigrants. However, by taking a broader view and considering national and global factors, we can dispel that rumor.

The end of the Cold War (1991) caused drastic changes in the United States that included the closing of major industries related to aerospace and defense. Financial institutions and real estate were severely affected and cost Californians hundreds of thousands of jobs. In addition to that, businesses in search of cheap, unregulated labor markets moved out of California in record numbers. This created a huge loss of jobs and revenue that is on-going and shows no sign of letting up.

Studies such as the one conducted by the Los Angeles County Internal Services Division (1992), claiming that legal and illegal immigrants used $808 million more in public services than they contributed through taxation, at first appear to support the allegations made by politicians. Upon closer examination, however, the study itself provides the reason for this discrepancy by noting that only 3.2 percent of the taxes paid by this population went to the County that is responsible for providing most of the services, while the Federal and State governments acquired the remainder (Fix and Passel, 1994).

In fact, several studies have clearly shown that immigrants use public health services for which they are eligible at a significantly lower rate than the general population. Undocumented immigrants are not entitled to re-

ceive unemployment, social security or disability benefits, although deductions are routinely withheld from their
paychecks. With the exception of emergency medical
care and Women, Infants and Children (WIC) nutrition
program benefits, they are ineligible for public assistance. In 1996, President Clinton signed the Federal
Welfare Reform Act which eliminates SSI and food
stamp benefits to legal immigrants (e.g. temporary visa
and green card holders, etc.) and grants the states the
option of refusing them other assistance programs and
non-emergency health care.

Immigration and How It Benefits
the United States

Mexican-Americans as well as immigrants from other
Spanish-speaking countries have contributed to the U.S
in various ways: from soldiers and heroes to braceros,
from labor union to mutual aid organizers and civil rights
activists. Their achievements in the fine arts have
earned them Academy, Emmy and Grammy Awards as

well as the Pulitzer and Nobel Prize. Many are well regarded as intellectuals in such fields as education, medicine, science and philosophy. They have been active in local, state and national politics—ranging from Senators to Ambassadors to Supreme Court Justices and have excelled in nearly every athletic sport in both the Olympic and professional levels.

Legal and illegal immigrants continue to augment the United States economy by providing low cost labor, tax revenue and by their participation as consumers, investors and entrepreneurs. The amount of money factory owners save by using immigrant labor has in some cases made the difference between keeping their factories operational or shutting them down. Without the availability of local cheap labor, owners often resort to the alternative means of keeping costs down—outsourcing, which in the long run may hurt the national economy even more. The cost of produce and services will also rise significantly without immigrant labor.

Most immigrants, after they have been in the labor force for a few years, either move up the ladder or start their own business. According to a Migration Policy Institute publication, *Immigration and America's Future: A New Chapter,* Hispanic-owned businesses continue to outpace the national average by a 3:1 ratio, while the number of Asian-owned businesses have grown at twice the national average.

An article titled, *Hispanic-Owned Businesses Booming,* written by Liz Marlantes for ABC News, states that "Between 1997 and 2002, the number of businesses owned by Hispanics grew by 31 percent—three times the national average for all businesses—hitting 1.6 million in 2002 and generating some $222 billion in revenue." She continues by commenting that, "Many of these businesses are cropping up in unexpected places. While most are still in California, Texas, Florida and New York, the states where Hispanic-owned firms are growing at the fastest rate, after New York, are Rhode Island and Georgia, followed by Nevada and South Carolina."

In addition to starting up businesses, Hispanic immigrants contribute to the U.S. economy by their purchasing power. According to HispanTelligence® (a division of Hispanic Business, Inc.) the analysis of data released by the U.S. Bureau of Economic Analysis, shows that in

2004, "U.S. Hispanic purchasing power has surged to nearly $700 billion and is projected to reach as much as $1 trillion by 2010." (See graph page 90.) "During the past decade, the rate of growth was more than two times the overall national rate. HispanTelligence® estimates current Hispanic purchasing power to be at 9.3 percent of the total current U.S. purchasing power and projects it to be 12 percent by 2015."

A phenomenon that began shortly after World War II continues to unfold as the "baby boomers" shift from the workforce to retirement in record numbers. Economists predict a huge decrease in the labor force at the same time that a demand for new jobs will arise, especially in the health care and service sectors. The Bureau of Labor Statistics estimates a demand for 56 million new jobs will exist by 2012, with approximately 75 million Americans retiring. The demand for laborers will increase proportionally.

Nevertheless, the financial state of the economy and the emotional reaction resulting from that, rather than careful consideration, seems to affect changes in attitude and the consequent enactment of new immigration laws. The simple fact that America would be hard-pressed to maintain its present economic status quo without immigrant labor, is drowned by the loud and strident voice of emotional rhetoric.

As the largest minority in the United States, Latinos are having an enormous economical, social and political impact on American society. Their influence, along with their numbers, will continue to increase in the coming decades.

U.S. Hispanic Purchasing Power

HispanTelligence®, *U.S Hispanic Purchasing Power: 1978-2010*

Immigration in the 21st Century and the Browning of America

According to the most recent national census (2000) there are 28 million foreign-born persons residing in the United States. Although in absolute numbers this represents the highest figure ever, it amounts to only 10.4 percent of the population compared to nearly 15 percent between 1870 to 1920. The impact of immigration on the labor market during the early part of the twentieth century was much greater than it is at the present time. In order for the labor market to be similarly impacted today, immigration would have to increase dramatically!

Rather than increasing, however, the current number of immigrants to the United States from Mexico is diminishing noticeably according to a survey completed in 2009 by the Pew Hispanic Center (see graph page 95). Survey data from the U.S. and Mexico reveal that in recent years a large flow of migrants back to Mexico has taken place. However, the size of the annual return flow appears to be stable since 2006. As for immigration to the U.S. from Mexico, surveys from both countries attest to recent substantial decreases in the number of new arrivals. This finding is reinforced by U.S. Border Patrol data showing markedly reduced apprehensions of Mexicans trying to cross into the United States illegally.

The immigration controversy is presently being viewed through the lens of a post 9/11 perspective and the current economic downturn. The lingering fear and tightened security are causing the nation to reconsider and redefine its laws once again. United States citizens who are currently unemployed are beginning to resent the immigrant who has a job. Whether the unemployed would actually do the work that the immigrant is doing seems to be of little concern. The belief that America's traditions and customs are being threatened by the influx of immigrants is on the rise. The current state of the economy, high unemployment rates and foreclosures are exacerbating feelings of fear and paranoia.

Arizona Governor Jan Brewer signed a bill (SB1070) into law on April 23, 2010 that makes being in Arizona illegally a state crime. The new law requires local police officers to question residents regarding their immigration status if there is reason to believe that they are illegal immigrants and are suspected of criminal behavior. The law also allows government agencies to be sued if they hinder the enforcement of immigration laws and makes hiring illegal immigrants for day labor a crime against the state.

The day before the bill was signed into law President Obama called it "misguided" and requested that the Justice Department examine it to see if it is legal. He also stated that enacting immigration reform is the responsibility of the federal government.

Mexico stated that the new law could affect cross-border relations. Mexican Foreign Secretary Patricia Espinosa said that her country would need to "consider whether the cooperation agreements that have been developed with Arizona are viable and useful."

The Mexican American Legal Defense and Education Fund plans to challenge the legality of the law and the National Coalition of Latino Clergy and Christian Leaders Legal Defense Fund is planning a federal lawsuit against Arizona to prevent the law from being applied. The biggest fear among protestors and Latino advocacy groups seems to be racial profiling and an increase in police brutality.

On July 6, 2010, the Obama administration filed a lawsuit against Arizona over the new immigration law. The Department of Justice lawsuit charges that the Arizona law conflicts with federal law and would interfere with immigrant enforcement and lead to police aggression toward those who are unable to prove their legal status.

Former New Mexico Governor Toney Anaya believes the reason immigrants are being blamed for the economic recession in California is due to "the uneasiness of society with the browning of America and the fact that Hispanics (are) the nations largest minority group." Pat Buchanan, talk show host and former presidential contender, confirms that fear with his view on immigration: "More immigrants mean more social friction and the slow erosion of the English speaking hybrid European culture we call America."

On the other hand, a growing number of US citizens, especially among the young and educated, welcome the new ideas and innovations that newcomers bring, especially since the majority of immigrants themselves tend to fall within the 15 to 35 age range.

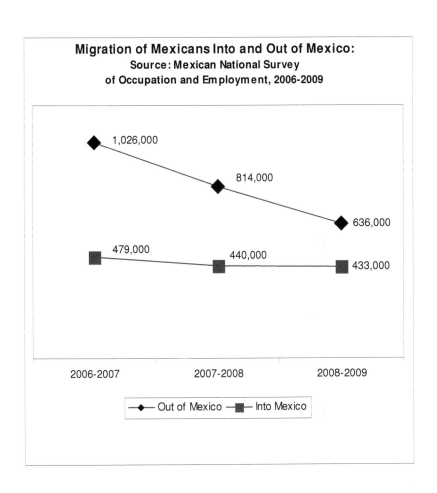

Migration of Mexicans Into and Out of Mexico:
Source: Mexican National Survey
of Occupation and Employment, 2006-2009

1,026,000

814,000

636,000

479,000

440,000

433,000

2006-2007   2007-2008   2008-2009

Out of Mexico —■— Into Mexico

Note: Figures reported are from February to February.
Source: Pew Hispanic Center: www.pewhispanic.org

95

Questions and Challenges

Fear of immigration comes in many shapes and many colors and shows itself in many forms. But what is it that we really fear? That the nation will be overrun and undermined by people with different theories and new concepts? Isn't that what made us a great nation? And if we are so great—why are we so afraid? Immigrants have been coming (and going) since the nation was born and we have yet to collapse under the weight of new ideas or become destroyed by innovation.

Perhaps the best way to bring the immigration issue to a size that we can better understand is to focus on individuality and humanity and not view immigrants as a massive tidal wave threatening our shores. After all, immigrants seek the very things that we as Americans have come to depend on: full time employment at competitive wages, adequate health care, public education, humane treatment as well as recognition and appreciation.

By helping our newest arrivals to become a part of the American success story we will strengthen the foundation upon which our nation was built—immigrants.

SECTION FIVE:
LATINOS AND EDUCATION

*"I am convinced that education
is the great equalizer."*

Jimmy Smits

School Segregation and Court Cases

In an article titled, *South by Southwest: Mexican Americans and Segregated Schooling, 1900-1950,* Vicki Ruiz points out that while not all school districts segregated Mexican youth, the fact that residential segregation existed caused educational segregation by default. However, it seems that most schools throughout the Southwest did participate in segregation. Historian Francisco Balderrama contends that at the start of the Great Depression "more than 80 percent of the school districts in southern California [sic] enrolled Mexicans and Mexican Americans in segregated schools." Additionally, the curriculum in "Mexican" schools focused on vocations. The general consensus among teachers and administrators was that the students had few ambitions and even fewer abilities apart from manual labor and domestic work.

According to Ruiz, prior to 1931 Mexican-American and White-American children in Lemon Grove, California, a small agricultural community near San Diego, attended the same school. However, in January of 1931 the school board decided to construct a separate facility for Mexican pupils. The two-room building resembled a barn and was equipped with used furniture, supplies and books. The parents of the students objected and formed a committee, *el Comité de Vecinos de Lemon Grove*. They voted to boycott the school and seek legal recourse. With the assistance of the Mexican Consul, the committee hired attorneys and filed a lawsuit, *Alvarez v. Lemon Grove School District*. The board members attempted to justify their actions on the grounds that a separate facility was needed in order to better meet the needs of non-English-speaking children. After hearing the case, District Judge Claude Chambers ordered the "immediate reinstatement" of Mexican children to their old school.

Over a decade later, in 1945, Gonzalo Mendez along with four other parents filed a class action lawsuit against four Orange County school districts in California when their children were not allowed to enroll in an all-white school. The case became know as *Mendez v. Westminster*. In 1946, the presiding judge, Paul McCormick, ruled in favor of the plaintiffs despite huge opposition.

McCormick stated that refusing Mexican-American children access to the schools violated the 14th constitutional amendment which states that all persons are entitled to equal protection and due process. The governor of California, Earl Warren, lobbied the California State legislature requesting the enactment of new legislation that would repeal the state's educational codes that permitted segregation in public schools. He eventually became the Chief Justice of the United States Supreme Court and was involved in overturning the "separate but equal doctrine" that marked the end of segregation in public schools nationwide when the *Brown v. Board of Education* case came before the Supreme Court in the 1950's.

The *Alvarez v. Lemon Grove School District* and the *Mendez v. Westminster* cases were not only successful in challenging the practice of segregation in California public schools, they also established an important legal precedent for the *Brown v. Board of Education* case.

From Segregation to Bilingual Education

Historically, Mexican-Americans have suffered racial prejudice throughout the Southwest including segregation from theaters, swimming pools, restrooms, drinking fountains and public schools. Most schools that permitted integration had a strict rule that prohibited the students from speaking Spanish on school grounds. Students who failed to comply were reprimanded or punished severely. In addition, they were frequently assigned to classes for low achievers, obligated to repeat grades and sometimes categorized as mentally deficient due to their limited English-speaking ability or other cultural differences.

The introduction of bilingual education in public schools during the late 1960's was a major turning point. Since its inception, politicians and educators have gone back and forth, not quite sure what to do about the bilingual/English-only issue. The following timeline put together by Jill Kerper Mora, Ed.D., provides an overview of the history of bilingual education in California.

Legal History of Bilingual Education in California

1967 Governor Ronald Reagan signs SB 53, the legislation allowing the use of other languages of instruction in California public schools. This bill overturned the 1872 law requiring English-only instruction.

1974 Chacón-Moscone Bilingual-Bicultural Education Act established transitional bilingual education programs to meet the needs of limited English proficient (LEP) students. Program requirements follow federal guidelines for identification, program placement and reclassification of students as fluent English proficient (FEP).

1981 Bilingual Education Act strengthened, spelling out in great detail the obligations of school districts to language minority students.

1986 Governor Deukmejian vetoes AB 2813 to extend the bilingual education into law.

1987 Governor Deukmejian again rejects a reauthorization bill and the bilingual education law is allowed to expire. The Sunset Provisions of the law go into effect. School districts continue to enforce the provisions of Chacón-Moscone without a clear mandate to do so.

1996 Four school districts in California are granted "waivers" by the State Board of Education exempting them from compliance with the provisions of the Bilingual Education Act. The waivers allowed the districts to establish "sheltered English immersion" programs and to dismantle their bilingual education programs.

1997 The Orange Unified School District is sued in California State Court in Sacramento in *Quiroz et al. vs. State Board of Education* by plaintiffs claiming that LEP students' rights are violated by the school district waivers for English-only instruction.

3/1998 Judge Robie rules that the State Board of Education was not authorized to grant waivers to the expired Bilingual Education Act. Further, the ruling stated that Orange Unified School District did not have to provide bilingual education under California law; only federal legal requirements for educating language minority children applied.

5/1998 Governor Pete Wilson vetoes Senate Bill 6. SB 6 contained many of the provisions of the Chacón-Moscone law but granted flexibility to school districts to use bilingual education or English immersion according to local needs and preferences.

6/1998 Passage of Proposition 227 virtually banning bilingual education except under certain special conditions and establishing a one-year "sheltered immersion" program for all LEP students.

Jill Kerper Mora, Ed.D., San Diego State University
http://edweb.sdsu.edu/people/jmora/pages/historybe.htm

Latinos and Education

Learning is intimately connected to life and begins the moment we enter the world. Education equips us with skills and helps us to develop new interests, explore different avenues and confronts us with a myriad of challenges and opportunities. It enhances our quality of life by enabling us to look at the world and the people in it through a perspective we might not otherwise have and gives us the opportunity to contribute to a changing and expanding world.

The following study regarding Latinos and education conducted by the White House Initiative on Educational Excellence, and the report that follows which explains the gap in attainment by Mark Lopez (Pew Hispanic Center) have been included in order to provide a reference point concerning Latinos' involvement in the educational system and the challenges the community faces as it strives to improve.

Latinos in School: Some Facts and Findings

ERIC Clearinghouse on Urban Education

(ERIC Digest # 162)

The number of Latino children and youth in public schools in the U.S. is steadily increasing. Currently, one third of the Latino population is under age 18. Latino students comprise 15 percent of K-12 students overall, a proportion projected to increase to 25 percent by 2025. Although Latinos have high aspirations, their educational attainment is consistently lower than that of other students. Latino student achievement is compromised by a variety of factors, including poverty, lack of participation in preschool programs, attendance at poor quality elementary and high schools, and limited English proficiency.

In order to help education policy and decision makers better respond to the strengths and challenges of the growing Latino school population, this digest presents key information about the current educational status of Latino students. One of an ERIC Clearinghouse on Urban Education series consisting of facts about specific student groups, the digest is based on Latinos in Education, a report by the White House Initiative on Educational Excellence for Hispanic Americans. The report, fully cited at the end of the digest, contains additional statistics as well as sources for the information.

Latinos in Preschool

Latinos under age 5 are less likely to be enrolled in early childhood education programs than other groups: 20 percent, as compared with 44 percent of African Americans and 42 percent of whites. Urban and suburban rates for Latinos are nearly the same.

The enrollment of Latino children in preschool increases with increases in parent educational attainment. Fewer Hispanics age 25 or older complete high school than do African Americans and whites, however. Enrollment also increases along with increases in family income. But here, too, Latinos, with a median family income of $28,000, lag behind the $39,000 median income of the population at large.

While 36 percent of Latino children live in poverty, only 26 percent attend Head Start programs, which are designed to remedy the effects of poverty on educational achievement.

Although children three to five years old may start school better prepared to learn if they are read to, only 65 percent of Latino children are read to, compared to 75 percent of African Americans and 90 percent of whites. Seventy percent of preschool teachers assert that they are not fully prepared to meet the needs of students with limited English proficiency or from diverse cultural backgrounds. Such lack of preparation can seriously impede the quality of Latino children's preschool education.

Latinos in Elementary School

Enrollment :

The enrollment of Latinos in elementary schools increased 157 percent between 1978 and 1998. Latinos comprise 15 percent of the elementary school-age population.

Nearly 50 percent of Latinos attend urban schools. They comprise one-quarter of the student population in central city schools.

Latino students attend schools with more than twice as many poor classmates as those attended by white students: 46 percent compared with 19 percent.

Educational Achievement :

Disparities between Latino students and others begin as early as kindergarten and remain through age 17. Latinos perform below their non-Hispanic peers in reading, mathematics, and science proficiency by age 9. Overall, they consistently perform below the national average in the National Assessment of Educational Progress (NAEP).

Latinos comprise three-quarters of all students enrolled in Limited English Proficient (LEP) programs, although not all Latino students have limited English proficiency.

Fewer Latinos than other students have access to a computer at home or school, despite the fact that computers are an essential tool: 68 percent use a computer at school (compared with 70 percent of African Americans and 84 percent of whites), and only 18 percent use one at home (compared with 19 percent of African Americans and 52 percent of whites).

Teachers:

Only about 4 percent of public school teachers are Latinos, whereas Latinos constitute 15 percent of the student body.

Latinos in Secondary School

Enrollment:

Latinos in grades 9-12 constitute 13 percent of the school population. By 2030, they are expected to comprise 23 percent of the population. * More than one-third of Latinos age 15 to 17 are enrolled below grade level, an unfortunately large number given the fact that enrollment below grade level is the highest predictor of dropping out.

Educational Achievement:

The average 1996 NAEP scores for Hispanic students age 17 were well below those of their white peers in reading, mathematics, and science.

Latino students earn more credits in computer science, foreign languages, and English than other groups; and fewer credits than other groups in history, science, and mathematics.

College Preparation:

The percentage of Latino seniors planning to attend a four-year college doubled from 24 percent in 1972 to 50 percent in 1992. The percentage intending to attend a two-year program increased from 12 to 20 percent.

Latino students are at least three times as likely to take a foreign language Advanced Placement (AP) examination as whites, and five times as likely as whites to be eligible for college credit from these tests. (White students are, though, more likely than either Latinos or African Americans to take AP examinations in all other subject areas.)

Only 35 percent of Latino students are enrolled in college preparatory or academic programs that provide access to four-year colleges or rigorous technical schools, as compared with 43 percent of African Americans and 50 percent of whites.

Moreover, Latino students are more frequently tracked into general courses that satisfy only the basic requirements: 50 percent are enrolled in general programs, as compared with 40 percent of African Americans and 39 percent of whites.

<u>Educational Attainment:</u>

The high school completion rate for Latinos has remained steady over several years: only 63 percent, as compared with 81 percent for African Americans and 90 percent for whites.

The dropout rate for Latinos is much higher than for other groups: in 1998, 30 percent of all Latino 16-through 24-years-old (1.5 million) were dropouts, whereas the dropout rate was 14 percent for African Americans and 8 percent for whites.

The high Latino dropout rate is partly attributable to the relatively greater dropout rate for Hispanic immigrants: 44 percent, as compared with 21 percent for the U.S. born.

The high school completion rate for Latino parents is increasing, but remains low. Up from 23 percent in 1972 to 45 percent in 1997, the completion rate for Latino parents still lags well below the rate for whites (90 percent), however. (Parental high school completion is an important factor in the educational attainment of their children.)

Latinos in College

Undergraduate Enrollment:

Latinos now represent almost 10 percent of the total student enrollment in higher education. They comprise 14.5 percent of the traditional college-age population in the U.S., a proportion expected to rise to 22 percent by 2025.

The representation of Latinos in higher education has grown dramatically, increasing 202 percent between 1976 and 1996.

Latinos enroll in college immediately upon high school graduation at a rate similar to that of other groups: 66 percent, compared with 60 percent for African Americans and 68 percent for whites. The enrollment rate for Latino high school completers age 18-24 over time is lower than that for other groups: 36 percent, compared with 40 percent for African Americans and 46 percent for whites.

The majority of Latino undergraduates (53 percent) are enrolled in two-year colleges, whereas the majority of African American (51 percent) and white (56 percent) undergraduates are enrolled in four-year colleges.

A higher percentage of Latino students (45 percent) are enrolled part time than either African Americans (40 percent) or whites (39 percent). Latinos (35 percent) are also more likely than African Americans (32 percent) or whites (25 percent) to take more than six years to earn a bachelor's degree.

Latino enrollment in undergraduate education is concentrated in the fewer than 200 colleges known as Hispanic-Serving Institutions (HSIs). HSIs are accredited degree-granting public or private non-profit higher education institutions with at least 25 percent total undergraduate Hispanic full-time equivalent student enrollment.

Undergraduate Educational Attainment

Latinos have doubled their undergraduate degree attainment since 1976. Twenty years later, Latino students earned 5 percent of all bachelor's degrees and 7 percent of all associate's degrees.

The top three disciplines for the bachelor's degrees of Latinos are business, social sciences, and education. The top disciplines for associate's degrees are liberal arts, business, and the health professions.

Graduate Enrollment

Latinos have increased their enrollment in graduate education, although they still comprise a smaller proportion of students than other groups: 4 percent, as compared with 6 percent for African Americans and 73 percent for whites. Within the Latino graduate student group, 60 percent were women in 1996.

Financial Aid

Latinos borrow less than other groups to pay for their education. Nearly 50 percent of first-year college students received grants and fewer than 30 percent received loans. In comparison, close to 60 percent of African Americans got grants and 42 percent got loans, and 46 percent of whites got grants and 31 percent got loans.

Faculty

In 1992 Latinos comprised fewer than 3 percent of full-time instructional faculty and staff in higher education.

The White House Initiative on Educational Excellence for Hispanic Americans.
Latinos in education: Early childhood, elementary, secondary, undergraduate, graduate.
ERIC Clearinghouse on Urban Education (ERIC Digest #162).

Latinos and Education:
Explaining the Attainment Gap

By Mark Hugo Lopez, Associate Director, Pew Hispanic Center

This report was prepared for the Latino Children, Families, & Schooling National Conference sponsored jointly by the Education Writers Association, the Pew Hispanic Center & the National Panel on Latino Children & Schooling (2009).

Nearly nine-in-ten (89%) Latino young adults ages 16 to 25 say that a college education is important for success in life, yet only about half that number (48%) say that they themselves plan to get a college degree, according to a new national survey of 2,012 Latinos ages 16 and older by the Pew Hispanic Center conducted from Aug. 5 to Sept. 16, 2009. (See graph page 123.)

The biggest reason for the gap between the high value Latinos place on education and their more modest aspirations to finish college appears to come from financial pressure to support a family, the survey finds.

Nearly three-quarters (74%) of all 16 to 25-year-old survey respondents who cut their education short during or right after high school say they did so because they had to support their family. Other reasons include poor English skills (cited by about half of respondents who cut short their education), a dislike of school and a feeling that they don't need more education for the careers they want (each cited by about four-in-ten respondents who cut their education short).

Latino schooling in the U.S. has long been characterized by high dropout rates and low college completion rates. Both problems have moderated over time, but a persistent educational attainment gap remains between Hispanics and whites.

When asked why Latinos on average do not do as well as other students in school, more respondents in the Pew Hispanic Center survey blame poor parenting and poor English skills than blame poor teachers. The explanation that Latino students don't work as hard as other students is cited by the fewest survey respondents; fewer than four-in-ten (38%) see that as a major reason for the achievement gap.

Si Se Puede!

Although the statistics quoted in the preceding pages show a dramatic increase in the number of Latinos enrolled in college during the latter half of the 20th century, there is still ample room for improvement.

Second and third generation Latinos are hopeful about their upward mobility. Their parents are equally optimistic; approximately 75 percent of them believe their children will achieve greater financial success than they themselves. However, it is not enough to be optimistic about the future or have high aspirations without action. Equality and fairness can only be accomplished through monumental and sustained commitment to higher learning and active participation in the social and political arenas.

According to more recent statistics (Pew Hispanic Center, 12/09) Latinos are both the largest and youngest ethnic group residing in the United States. One-out-of-five school children and one-out-of-four newborns are Latinos. This is the first time in U.S. history that an ethnic group of this size has made up so large a share of its youth. The attitudes, values, social behavior, family involvement, economic status, etc. are all factors that play an important role in determining the direction and ultimate outcome of Latino youth in today's society.

The decisions and life choices that such a vast number of people make as they grow into adulthood will impact the type of society the United States will become in the 21st century.

A College Education Is Important

Question: "In order to get ahead in life these days,
it's necessary to get a collee education." (% who agree)

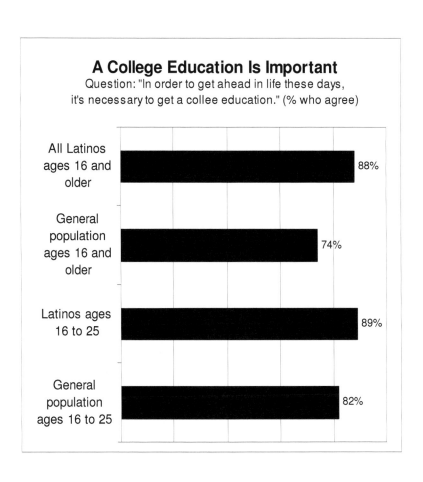

All Latinos
ages 16 and
older — 88%

General
population
ages 16 and
older — 74%

Latinos ages
16 to 25 — 89%

General
population
ages 16 to 25 — 82%

Latinos and Education: Explaining the Attainment Gap
Pew Hispanic Center, 2009

APPENDIX

Graphs

Glossary of Terms

About the Author

Bibliography

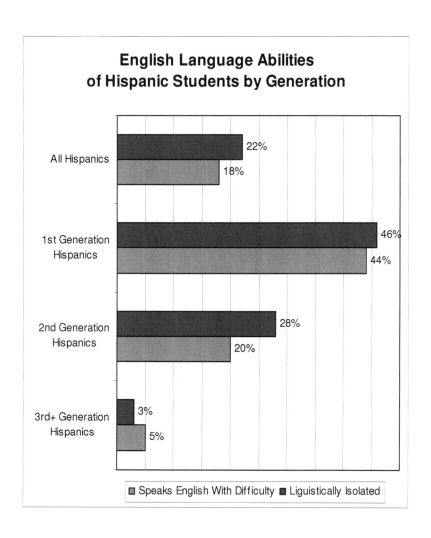

English Language Abilities of Hispanic Students by Generation

All Hispanics
- 22%
- 18%

1st Generation Hispanics
- 46%
- 44%

2nd Generation Hispanics
- 28%
- 20%

3rd+ Generation Hispanics
- 3%
- 5%

☐ Speaks English With Difficulty ■ Liguistically Isolated

The Census Bureau identifies as linguistically isolated all members of households in which either no person over the age of 13 speaks only English at home or no person over the age of 13 who speaks a language other than English at home speaks English "very well."

One-in-Five and Growing Fast: A Profile of Hispanic School Students
Pew Hispanic Center

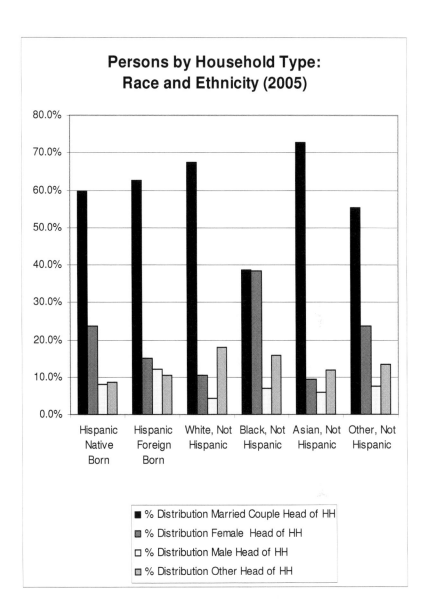

Persons by Household Type: Race and Ethnicity (2005)

Legend:
- ■ % Distribution Married Couple Head of HH
- ▨ % Distribution Female Head of HH
- ☐ % Distribution Male Head of HH
- ▨ % Distribution Other Head of HH

2005 American Community Survey
Pew Hispanic Center

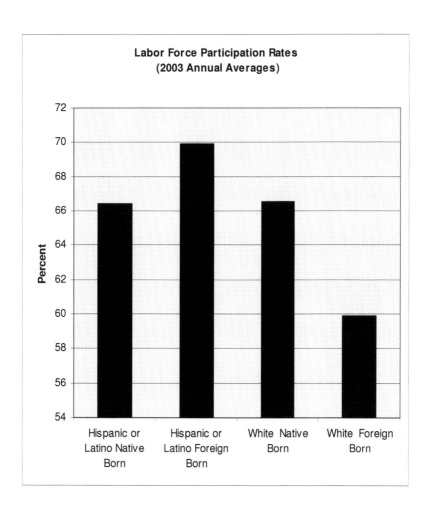

Labor Force Participation Rates
(2003 Annual Averages)

US Bureau of Labor Statistics
http://www.bls.gov/opub/mlr/2004/06/ressum.pdf

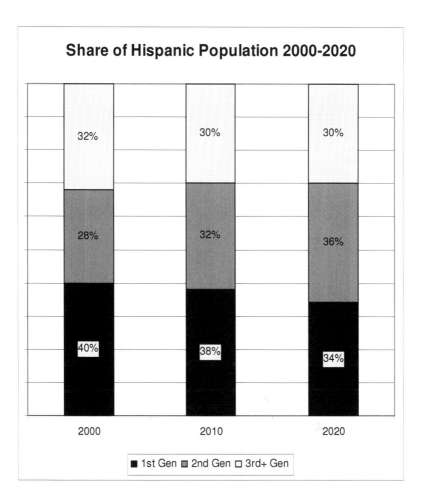

Share of Hispanic Population 2000-2020

	2000	2010	2020
3rd+ Gen	32%	30%	30%
2nd Gen	28%	32%	36%
1st Gen	40%	38%	34%

■ 1st Gen ▨ 2nd Gen ☐ 3rd+ Gen

The Rise of the Second Generation: Changing Patterns in Hispanic Population Growth
Pew Hispanic Center

GLOSSARY

American G.I. Forum: A Congressionally-chartered Hispanic veterans and civil rights organization. AGIF currently operates chapters throughout the United States, with a focus on veteran's issues, education, and civil rights.

Agricultural Workers Organizing Committee (AWOC): An organization sponsored by the National AFL-CIO for the purpose of organizing farm workers. Composed mostly of Filipino workers, AWOC called a grape strike in Delano on September 8, 1965. Two weeks later, the NFWA joined the strike.

Bracero Program: A series of laws and diplomatic agreements, initiated by an August 1942 exchange of diplomatic notes between the United States and Mexico, for the importation of temporary contract laborers from Mexico to the United States.

Califorñios: A term used to identify a Californian of Latin American descent, regardless of race, during the period that California was part of the Viceroyalty of New Spain, governed from Mexico City.

Confederation de Uniones de Campesinos y Obreros Mexicanos (CUCOM): In the early 1930s, Chicanos established some 40 agricultural unions in California. The CUCOM was the largest and ultimately included 50 local chapters and 5,000 members. Most of the unions created during this time period later joined the American Federation of Labor or the Congress of Industrial Organizations.

Immigration Reform and Control Act: An Act of Congress which reformed United States immigration law. The Act made it illegal to knowingly hire or recruit illegal immigrants (immigrants who do not possess lawful work authorization), required employers to attest to their employees' immigration status, and granted amnesty to certain illegal immigrants who entered the United States before January 1, 1982 and had resided there continuously.

Hispanic Serving Institution (HSI): A term used for a Federal program designed to assist Colleges or Universities in the United States that attempt to assist first generation, low income Hispanic students.

Manifest Destiny: The 19th century belief that the United States was destined to expand across the North American continent, from the Atlantic seaboard to the Pacific Ocean.

Movimiento Estudiantil Chicano de Aztlán (MEChA): An organization that seeks to promote Chicano unity and empowerment through education and political action.

Presidio: A fortified base established by the Spanish and Mexicans in North America between the sixteenth and nineteenth centuries.

Rancheros: The Spanish, and later the Mexican, government encouraged settlement of Alta California by the establishment of large land grants, many of which were later turned into ranchos, devoted to the raising of cattle and sheep.

Tejanos: (Spanish for "Texan"; archaic spelling Texano) is a term used to identify a Texan of Mexican and/or Latin-American descent.

Treaty of Guadalupe Hidalgo: The peace treaty, largely dictated by the United States to the interim government of a militarily occupied Mexico, that ended the Mexican-American War (1846–1848). From the standpoint of the U.S., the treaty provided for the Mexican cession of 1.36 million km² (525,000 square miles) to the United States in exchange for $15 million (equivalent to $380 million today). From the standpoint of Mexico, the treaty included an additional 1,007,935 km² (389,166 sq mi) as Mexico had never recognized the Republic of Texas nor its annexation by the U.S., and Mexico lost 55% of its pre-war territory. The treaty also ensured safety of existing property rights of Mexican citizens in the transferred territories. Despite assurances to the contrary, property rights of Mexican citizens were often not honored by the United States.

Zoot Suit: A suit with high-waisted, wide-legged, tight-cuffed, pegged trousers, and a long coat with wide lapels and wide padded shoulders.

Zoot Suit Riots: The Zoot Suit Riots were a series of riots that erupted in Los Angeles, California during World War II, between White sailors and Marines stationed throughout the city and Latino youths, who were recognizable by the zoot suits they favored.

ABOUT THE AUTHOR

Paulina Rael Jaramillo was born and raised in New Mexico where her family roots are deeply entrenched. In 1598 her ancestors migrated to North America and in 1610 helped establish the settlement known today as Santa Fe. However, most of her adult life has been spent in California where her children and grandchildren reside.

Her writing career began in 1991 as a contributing writer for a regional newspaper and a freelance writer for national magazines. She has currently contributed to eight inspirational books and co-authored a one-act play that was performed on stage. Her most recent published work includes a set of two books titled, *A Time to Heal; Grief Recovery Guide and Workbook* (2008) and a follow up book titled, *Life Interrupted: Grief Recovery Guide and Workbook* (2009). She has a Master of Arts degree in Rehabilitation Counseling from California State University San Bernardino.

Author contact information:

Website: paulinajaramillo.com
Email: paulinajaramillo@charter.net

BIBLIOGRAPHY

Bogardus, Emory, *Mexican in the United States*, University of Southern California Press, Los Angeles, 1934.

Camarillo, Albert, *Chicanos in California*, Boyd and Fraser Publishing Co., San Francisco, 1984.

Carrigan, William D. & Clive Webb, "The Lynching of Persons of Mexican Origin or Descent in the United States, 1848 to 1928", In *Journal of Social History,* Vol 37, pp. 411-438. George Mason University Press, Fairfax, VA, 2003.

Davis, Marilyn P., *Mexican Voices/American Dreams*, Henry Holt & Co., New York, 1990.

ERIC Clearinghouse on Urban Education, The White House Initiative on Educational Excellence for Hispanic Americans, "Latinos in education: Early childhood, elementary, secondary, undergraduate, graduate", In *ERIC Digest* #162, Washington, D.C., 2001.

Fix, Michael and Jeffrey Passel, *Immigration and Immigrants: Setting the Record Straight,* The Urban Institute, Washington, D.C., http://www.urban.org/publications/ 305184.html#V, 1994.

Fry, Richard and Felisa Gonzales, *One-in-Five and Growing Fast: A Profile of Hispanic Public School Students*, Pew Hispanic Center, Washington, D.C., http://pewhispanic.org/files/ reports/92.pdf, 2009.

Gann, L.H.,& Peter J. Dunigan, *The Hispanics in the United States*, Westview Press, Boulder, CO,1987.

HispanTelligence®, *Hispanic Purchasing Power: Projections to 2015,* Hispanic Business, Inc., Santa Barbara, CA, https://secure.hbinc.com/product/view.asp?id=222, 2005.

HispanTelligence®, *U.S. Hispanic Purchasing Power: 1978-2010,* Hispanic Business, Inc., Santa Barbara, CA, http://www.hispanic business.com/news/2004/5/5/hispanic_purchasing_power_ surges_to_700.htm, 2004.

Hunt, Kasie, "Some Stories Hard to Get in History Books", *USA Today,* McLean, VA, http://www.usatoday.com/news/education/2006-04-04-history-books_x.htm, 2006.

Langely, Lester D., *MexAmerican: Two Countries, One Future,* Crown Publishing, New York, 1988.

League of United Latin American Citizens, *LULAC History,* Washington, D.C., http://www.lulac.org/about/history/, 2010.

Liberal Arts Instructional Services: Texas Politics, *Voting, Campaigns and Elections: Historical Barriers to Voting,* University of Texas at Austin, 2nd Ed-Rev 24, http://texaspolitics.laits.utexas. edu/6_5_3.html, 2010.

Lopez, Mark Hugo, *Latinos and Education: Explaining the Attainment Gap,* Pew Research Center, Washington, D.C., pewhispanic. org/reports/report.php?ReportID=115, 2009.

Marlantes, Liz, *Hispanic-Owned Businesses Booming: Immigrant Population Growing and Moving to Unexpected States,* ABC News, New York, http://abcnews.go.com/US/story?id=1752325&page=1, 2006.

Martinez, Oscar, "Hispanics in Arizona", In *Arizona at Seventy-Five: The Next Twenty-Five Years,* ed. Beth Luey and Noel J. Stone, Arizona State University, Public History Program and the Arizona Historical State Society, 1987.

Mora, Jill Kerper, *Legal History of Bilingual Education,* San Diego State University, San Diego, CA, http://edweb.sdsu.edu/people/ jmora/pages/historybe.htm, 2005.

Morin, Raul, *Among the Valiant*, Borden Publishing Co., Alhambra, CA, 1966.

Officer, James E., *Hispanic Arizona 1536-1856*, University of Arizona Press, Tucson, AZ, 1987.

Passel, Jeffrey and D'Vera Cohn, *Mexican Immigrants: How Many Come? How Many Leave?* Pew Hispanic Center, Washington, D.C., h*ttp://pewhispanic.org/reports/report.php?ReportID=112*, 2009.

Prago, Albert, *Strangers in Their Own Land: A History of Mexican-Americans,* Four Winds Press, New York, 1973.

Ruiz, Vicki I., "South by Southwest: Mexican Americans and Segregated Schooling, 1900-1950", In *Organization of American Historians (OAH) Magazine of History,* http://www.oah.org/pubs/magazine/deseg/ruiz.html, 2001.

Smith, Chuck, *Native Peoples of North America*, Cabrillo College, Aptos, CA, www.cabrillo.edu/~crsmith/southwest.html, 2002.

Torrez, Robert J., "1912-The Road to Statehood", In *New Mexico State Record Center and Archives*, New Mexico, http://www.new mexicohistory.org/filedetails_docs.php?fileID=21636, 2010.

United States General Accounting Office, *Treaty of Guadalupe Hidalgo: Definition and List of Community Land Grants in New Mexico*, Exposure Draft, Washington, D.C., http://www.gao.gov/new.items/d0 1330.pdf, 2001.

Vigil, Maurillo E., *Los Patrones: Profiles of Hispanic Political Leaders in New Mexico History*, University Press of America, Washington, D.C., 1980.

Williams, Norma, *The Mexican American Family: Traditions and Change*, General Hall Inc., New York, 1990.

Made in the USA
Charleston, SC
13 September 2010